jack russell terrier

understanding and
caring for your breed

Written by
Claire Horton-Bussey

jack russell terrier

understanding and
caring for your breed

Written by
Claire Horton-Bussey

Pet Book Publishing Company

Bishton Farm, Bishton Lane, Chepstow, NP16 7LG, United Kingdom.

881 Harmony Road, Unit A, Eatonton, GA31024 United States of America

Printed and bound in China through Printworks International

Every reasonable care has been taken in the compilation of this publication. The Publisher and Author cannot accept liability for any loss, damage, injury or death resulting from the keeping of Jack Russell Terriers by user(s) of this publication, or from the use of any materials, equipment, methods or information recommended in this publication or from any errors or omissions that may be found in the text of this publication or that may occur at a future date, except as expressly provided by law.

The 'he' pronoun is used throughout this book instead of the rather impersonal 'it', however no gender bias is intended.

ISBN: 978-1-906305-71-0
ISBN: 1-906305-71-4

Acknowledgements

The publishers would like to thank the following for help with photography:
Hilary Bowden and Gill Alcorn, Kirsten Bomke (The VixenWarren), Hannah and Lown Lougher, Shawn and Vicky Powell.

Photographs on pages 56, 57, 68 and 69 © Warren Photographic.

Contents

Introducing the Russell Terrier 8

Tracing back in time 16

Developing the breed 22

What should a Russell Terrier look like? 28

What do you want from your Russell? 36

What does your Russell want from you? 42

Extra considerations 48

    Male or female? 50

    More than one? 52

    Taking on an older dog 54

    Rescued dogs 54

Sourcing a puppy 56

Puppy watching 64

A Russell Terrier friendly home 70

Settling in 84

House training 94

Choosing a diet 98

Caring for your Russell Terrier 108

Social skills 126

Training guidelines 132

First lessons 136

Come when called 140

Stationary exercises 144

Control exercises 148

Opportunities for Russells 154

Health care 162

Common ailments 174

Inherited disorders 184

Introducing the Russell Terrier

What picture does the Russell Terrier conjure up in your mind? Is it a smart, sporty looking terrier that is predominantly white in color; is it a slightly bigger, more refined-looking dog, or is it a small, jaunty, short-legged dog that may have bigger patches of color on his white coat?

This question is not as daft as it sounds as there are, in fact, three types of terrier that have developed from the same root:

- **Parson Russell Terrier:** This is the bigger dog that is registered with Kennel Clubs and is exhibited in the show ring.

- **Jack Russell Terrier:** This looks broadly similar

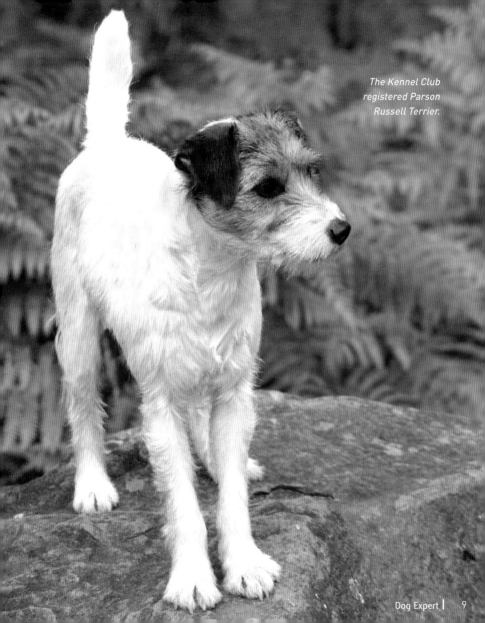

The Kennel Club registered Parson Russell Terrier.

to the Parson, but is built on working lines, and is not eligible for Kennel Club competition.

- **Pet Jack Russells:** The short-legged type which is a great favorite among pet owners.

Despite the physical differences, it is important to bear in mind that these three terrier types all come from the same source; they share a similar temperament and outlook on life, and require the same care and training. The similarities between them far outnumber the differences, so for the purposes of this book, we will refer to them all as Russell Terriers, unless there is a need to specifically identify the individual types.

Understanding terriers

Before we look more closely at the character of Russell Terriers, it is worth gaining an understanding of terriers in general. The name 'terrier' derives from 'terre', meaning earth/ground, and breeders over the centuries fine-tuned different types of dog to go to earth in search of quarry, such as fox and badger.

The Cairn Terrier, the Border Terrier, the West Highland White Terrier, and Russell Terriers were all developed for this purpose, and they share a fearless, determined temperament, suited to dogs that needed to face up to a much larger opponent. These feisty little terriers were also excellent ratters, and were much in demand for vermin control.

Although some terriers are still used for their original purpose, and thoroughly enjoy a day's hunting, the vast majority are pet dogs. They have adapted well to domestic life and make outstanding companions, but owners agree that the terrier side of their character is never far from the surface.

Terrier in body...

'Workmanlike' is an adjective often used to describe the Russell Terrier. He should be able to perform his original purpose as an earth dog, and, like any working terrier, he should be able to be spanned behind the shoulders. A dog with too big a chest won't be able to enter earth holes, and so the chest has traditionally been measured by using the hands. With the dog facing away from you, span the chest with your hands, just behind the elbows, with your thumbs at the top and your fingers meeting at the front of the chest. Of course, hand size varies, but an average pair of hands will span a circumference of about 14 inches (36 cm).

Parsons stand at about 14 inches (36 cm) to the withers for dogs and 13 inches (33 cm) for bitches, although smaller terriers can be shown, as it is accepted that such dogs are needed to work in certain fields. Regardless of height, the dog must be balanced, in proportion, and of good type.

Jack Russells of the working type are between 10 and 15 inches (25.5-38 cm). The pet-type has no standard height, coming in various sizes – and shapes! Some can be quite box-like, others are longer than they are tall.

The pet Jack Russell.

...and spirit

Regardless of type, Russell Terriers all share a larger-than-life personality. Loving pets with their family, they can instantly transform into little hunters and need a home where they can exercise their natural behavior.

Following their noses, hunting smells, investigating rabbit holes and chasing squirrels is their idea of doggie heaven and, despite their size, they are built for endurance and can hunt for hours without tiring.

Russell Terriers are also faster than you would think, with the ability to produce bursts of speed to catch their quarry – be it a rat, a squirrel, a blackbird in the garden, or their favorite squeaky toy!

Coat and colors

A workmanlike terrier needs a decent jacket to protect him from the elements and the environment. The coat keeps him warm and dry in wind, rain, and freezing temperatures, but it should also protect the skin from briars and other hazards in the undergrowth, including the teeth and claws of any quarry.

A Russell Terrier may be smooth-coated, broken-coated, or rough-coated. They are predominantly white, and the traditional markings over the eye and ears, with a spot at the root of the tail, are highly prized.

Tracing back in time

The history of some dog breeds is clouded in myth, mystery and legend, but with Russell Terriers, we have one man to thank for establishing the breed.

The Reverend John (aka Jack) Russell was a West Country clergyman, with a passion for hunting. He was born in Devon in 1795, and it was not long before he developed a taste for the outdoor life. When he was at school he spent so much time hunting with dogs that he was asked to leave!

Undeterred, John continued to hunt throughout his academic career, and it was when he was at Exeter College, Oxford, that a meeting took place that was to change his life. One day he was out walking and passed a milkman who was accompanied by a small terrier. He was struck by her "courage, endurance and hardihood" and knew he had to have her. After some negotiations with the milkman, Trump, as she

was called, was his – and the first chapter of the breed's history was complete.

Trump had a dense, wire coat, which was white in color, with a dark tan patch over her eyes, ears and at the base of her tail. In size, she was compared to a vixen, and her legs, according to Russell's biographer, E.W.L. Davies, were "as straight as arrows".

No records exist of the sires that were used, but it is known that Trump was the founding bitch of Russell's new line of hunting dogs and that she was his canine muse – the ideal to which he bred.

Bred to hunt

Once ordained, and back in Devon, Russell continued to breed and hunt, a pastime that was as much a vocation to him as the Church. He married Penelope in 1826, and settled as parson of Swymbridge in 1832. For most of the 45 years that Russell was in Swymbridge, he hunted (otter in the summer, fox in the winter) and fine-tuned his pack. His dogs had remarkable stamina, with reports of Trump and Tip (her descendant) running up to 20 miles on a hunt.

They were also bred to work on their own wits: anticipating where the quarry might appear, finding

Parson Russell established his own line of hunting terriers.

short-cuts on land they might never have hunted on before, and making split-second decisions without human direction. So when you are cursing your own Russell Terrier for escaping your Fort Knox-like garden or breaking into a biscuit tin that's been put into an 'unreachable' cupboard, remember your dog's ancestors.

We also have the Parson to thank for the Russell Terrier's obstinacy and vocal nature. Once quarry had been found, the dogs would bark to alert the accompanying hounds.

Russell Terriers are not yappy dogs; they generally bark only if they have something important to say. But once they do have news that they want to relay

– perhaps of a rat they have trapped behind a shed, or of a stranger near their territory – then they will woof for all they are worth! As for their boldness and tenacity, this also has deep-seated roots in the breed. Should the quarry go to ground, the terriers had to be courageous and tough enough to flush it out of its bolthole, so the hunt could resume.

The show world

In 1873 the Reverend Russell helped to found the Kennel Club, the world's first all-breed canine registry, and he judged terriers, unsurprisingly, at the first Kennel Club-sanctioned show the following year.

Interestingly – particularly for working enthusiasts who eschew the show ring – the Reverend did not exhibit his terriers as he believed there was a noticeable split, differentiating show and working dogs. He compared it to the difference between a wild flower and a cultivated garden rose. The working terrier fans continued with their unadulterated terrier, with the show Fox Terrier continuing in the show ring as quite a separate entity.

Facing page:
The pub sign in
Swymbridge. The
village is dedicated to
the memory of Parson
Russell and his terriers.

JACK RUSSELL

THE REV. JACK RUSSELL'S
(first terrier)

Developing the breed

The Reverend John Russell built up such a reputation for fine hunting dogs that fellow terrier fanatics were keen that his work should not be lost after his death. The first Parson Jack Russell Club was established in 1894, to promote the breeding of "the old-fashioned North Devon type of Fox Terrier, as bred and made famous by Reverend J. Russell."

The secretary of the club, Arthur Heinemann, continued to breed to the type created by the parson, sourcing as many direct descendants from the Reverend's pack as he could. Of course no breed or type can be saved single-handedly, so Heinemann wrote a Breed Standard in 1904, whereby others could breed to maintain the type. Heinemann's version was the basis of the Parson Jack Russell Terrier Standard

later submitted to the Kennel Club by the breed club.

Unfortunately, Heinemann didn't quite follow his own script. His love of badger digging (where a terrier finds a badger, which is dug out, put in a bag, weighed and released) resulted in him tweaking the Parson's terrier, breeding in some Bull Terrier to make the terriers stronger and more robust for the 'sport'. Russell Terriers with clear 'bull' heads are still visible today.

The Parson Jack Russell Terrier Club closed following the decline of the breed during the Second World War, although die-hard fans managed to maintain the breed in Devon, albeit in smaller numbers.

The short-legged Jack

All the time that the Parson Jack Russell Terrier was in decline, an offshoot of the breed was on the rise – the short-legged, pet Jack Russell. This dog was the result of the Parson's type of terrier crossed with all sorts of other breeds, including the Corgi, Yorkshire Terrier, Chihuahua, Lakeland Terrier, Fox Terrier, and the Staffordshire Bull Terrier. There were no restrictions to the 'ingredients' that went into the Jack Russell pot, as this dog was not – and still is not – registered with the Kennel Club and there was no breed club acting to ensure consistency amongst breeders.

That is not to say that the short-legged Jack Russell didn't have an enthusiastic following – a popularity that continues to this day. Although there are great variations, given his wide parentage, he is instantly recognizable as belonging to a type and is loved the world over.

Official recognition

Breed stalwarts were determined to maintain the type of dog developed by the Reverend John Russell, and their efforts finally paid off with the rebirth of the Parson Jack Russell Club in 1983. This was followed by Kennel Club in recognition 1990.

In 1999, the breed name was changed to Parson Russell Terrier – to emphasize the split with Jack Russells – and this is the official name for the Kennel Club registered breed.

The situation was confused in the USA as enthusiasts who were opposed to recognizing working Russells, registered 'Parson Jack Russell' as a trademark. This meant that the American Kennel Club had to use 'Jack Russell Terrier' when the breed was first registered in 1997. However, this was changed in 2003 so that all countries were using the same name – Parson Russell Terrier – for the longer legged show dog.

The Jack Russell may not have official Kennel Club recognition, but enthusiasts who favour the working type, have formed their own clubs. The Jack Russell Terrier Club of America was founded in 1976; it is the national registry for the breed as well as having its own Breed Standard. It also organizes trials where dogs can compete in the show ring and in terrier sports. The Jack Russell Terrier Club of Great Britain, founded in 1974, and the Jack Russell Club of Australia, founded in 1972, perform similar functions.

What should a Russell Terrier look like?

All purebred dogs have their own Breed Standard, which is, essentially, a picture in words describing the ideal specimen. This written blueprint of each breed is the standard by which each dog is judged in the show ring.

There is an official Kennel Club Standard for Parson Russell Terriers in the UK and an American Kennel Club Standard for the Parson Russell Terrier in the United States. There is also a Standard for the working-type Jack Russell Terrier, written by the Jack Russell Terrier Club of Great Britain, and also one by the Jack Russell Terrier Club of America (JRTCA).

Of course, the short-legged pet-type Jack Russell has no Breed Standard. They are shorter than their working and show cousins and, size-wise, they can range from the petite to the pretty hefty. Features, such as ear carriage and tail carriage, may vary, and they may have heavier markings than the other types.

Despite all these variations, the written Standards for show and working Russells are fairly similar. As you would expect, the Jack Russell Standards emphasize the working aspects of the breed, and stress the dog's function over aesthetics. However, the Parson Standards also pay tribute to the terrier's working ability – for example, permitting "honourable scars" and stating that this is "essentially a working terrier with ability and conformation to go to ground and run with hounds."

Here is a brief overview of the Russell Terrier – amalgamating all the points of the various Standards.

General appearance

This is a workmanlike, tough, active dog, always on the go. Honourable scars – those acquired from working – should not be frowned upon.

Characteristics and temperament

This working terrier should be able to do his original job – to run with hounds and go to ground. Fearless, happy, alert, and active, this dog should be confident – not aggressive or nervous.

Head and skull

The head/skull, which should be in proportion to the body, is flat, moderately wide at the ears and narrowing gradually to the eyes. The muzzle length from the nose to the stop should be slightly less than the distance from the stop to the occiput. The nose is black.

Below: The Russell Terrier should have the conformation and character of a working dog.

Eyes, ears, mouth

The almond-shaped, dark eyes are full of life and expression. The small, v-shaped, drop ears are carried forward, and the leather is moderately thick. The mouth has strong jaws and muscular cheeks. The strong teeth have a complete scissor-bite (where the top teeth closely overlap the lower ones).

Neck and forequarters

The clean, muscular neck is of good length and gradually widens to the shoulders, which are sloping, well laid back and cut cleanly at the withers. The legs are strong and straight-boned and turn neither in nor out. The elbows are perpendicular to the body and work free of the sides.

Body

The chest should be capable of being spanned behind the shoulder by average-sized hands. The ribs should not be over-sprung (nor should they be flat). The back should be strong and straight, and the loin is slightly arched.

Hindquarters

As befits a working dog, the hindquarters should be well-angulated, strong and muscular, to give good drive and propulsion when the dog is moving.

Feet

A hardy working dog who hunts through tough terrain needs strong boots! The pads should therefore be hard, and the feet should be round and compact, turning neither in nor out.

Tail

Traditionally the tail was docked; the length complementing the body – usually around 4 inches (10 cm) long which provided a good handhold for pulling the dogs out of holes. Docking is still permitted in the US, but this is not the case in the UK and much of Europe. The tail should be strong, set on high, and carried gaily when the dog is moving.

Gait/movement

This dog moves in a free, lively, co-ordinate manner, with a straight action, both in front and behind.

Coat and color

The coat must be harsh and dense – all over, including on the tummy, where in many breeds it is usually quite sparse. The skin, too, must be thick and loose, to offer protection. There are several coat varieties – rough, smooth or broken-coated (somewhere between rough and smooth, with a clean outline but a more 'ragged' appearance to the coat around the shoulders and neck).

Whatever the coat type, the hair is harsh and dense to offer protection against the undergrowth – and all weather conditions. Woolliness is not acceptable; it might look as if it would protect against the cold, but it would just retain wetness, rather than repel it.

Russell Terriers are predominantly white, usually with black or brown/tan markings, often confined to the head and/or base of the tail. Lemon markings can also occur.

Size

Size can range from 10 inches (25 cm) to 15 inches (38 cm) at the withers. An ideal height for Parson Russells is given as 14 inches (36 cm) for dogs and 13 inches (33 cm) for bitches, though it is recognized that smaller terriers are required for certain working conditions.

Right: The Russell is a predominantly white dog, with a harsh dense coat, which may be smooth, rough or broken.

What do you want from your Russell Terrier?

Affectionate, fun-loving, energetic, too intelligent for his own good sometimes, and also fearless to the point of stupidity – there really is no other dog like the Russell Terrier. But does he suit your lifestyle?

Family dog

This is a breed with an independent mind, stemming from the days when he had to work on his own initiative, but coupled with this is a real affinity with people. A Russell loves to be part of a family and included in all activities. He is loving and loyal, and will bond closely with the people in his life. He

seems to have a sixth sense and has a way of tuning into his owner's moods.

Most Russells get on well with children as they love the opportunity for extra playtimes. However, it is essential that children are taught how to behave so the dog is never teased, or over-stimulated to the point that he becomes uncontrollable.

Given careful supervision, particularly when a puppy first comes into your life, you will find that there is no better companion.

What type?

As highlighted, there are three types of Russell Terrier, and you need to decide which is the right one for you: show type, working type, or pet?

There is little difference in terms of character, but if you want to get involved in the Kennel Club show world, you need to go for a Parson Russell Terrier.

Jack Russell Terriers, bred from working lines, can be registered with their own breed clubs, but they are not eligible for KC shows. Pet Jack Russells – the short-legged variety – are perfect as pets, and for competing in a sport such as agility, but they do not have any form of official recognition.

Bear in mind that if you choose to go to a breeder that has a reputation for producing quality Parson Russell Terriers for the show ring, you are buying a dog with potential – not the finished article. The most promising puppy may develop a minor fault, which makes him unsuitable for showing, so you must be committed to giving your dog a home for life, regardless of how he turns out.

Below: Short-legged Jack Russells can vary considerably in appearance.

Working dogs

There are relatively few opportunities to work a Russell Terrier in his traditional hunting role, but if you live in a rural location – on a farm or where horses are kept – a Russell will take on the role of ratter with great distinction. This is not something that has to be taught; it is in his make-up.

However, if you want to bring out your Russell's working ability, it is best to direct him at one of the canine sports.

The Russell may not take competitive obedience seriously, but he is a top-class agility dog, and many have got right to the top in this sport. In the USA, where earth dog trials are staged, the Russell is a most enthusiastic competitor.

Most Russell Terriers love competing at Agility.

What does your Russell Terrier want from you?

A small-sized terrier will fit into most homes, and there is a temptation to choose a breed simply because it is a handy size with a reasonably low-maintenance coat. However, the Russell may be small in size but he is big on personality, and he needs an owner who will relish the challenge of this active, quick-witted breed.

Giving time

First and foremost, a Russell Terrier wants to spend time with you. No dog, of any breed, should be left for longer than four hours on his own, and this is most particularly true of a Russell.

Never happier than when he is at the hub of activity, a Russell will be quick to find his own agenda if he is left on his own. Make sure you spend quality time interacting with your dog, and he will reward you a hundred-fold.

Leadership

If you are inexperienced with dogs, or find it hard to be assertive, many Russells will run rings around you. This is a bold, confident breed – as most terriers are – and he respects strong leadership. If you are inconsistent about the house rules, or let him rule the roost, he will become a hooligan in no time. For a Russell, you need to have some Russell personality traits yourself: strength, determination, fun, and a little bit of feistiness...

Below: Regardless of the weather, a Russell Terrier needs plenty of exercise.

Exercise

The Russell is a hardy breed that is used to the elements, and needs two good walks a day, come rain or shine.

This is not a dog that will be happy with a quick walk around the block. Ideally, for an adult, two hour-long off-lead romps in a wood or safe, enclosed park, are needed. Some are happy with less, particularly if elderly, but most will want even more.

If you are not a walker, then another breed, such as a Chihuahua or a Pug, may be a more suitable choice.

Stimulation

Exercise on its own is not enough for a Russell Terrier. This is a lively, intelligent dog that needs ongoing training to keep his busy mind ticking over. If he's bored he will quickly find a way to amuse himself – be it chasing the cat, de-stuffing your finest cushions, or working out how to empty your kitchen bin or fridge!

You will need to go to regular puppy classes with your youngster, and adult training classes are also advised to keep your Russell mentally stimulated and, importantly, under your control.

Care and attention

The Russell is a relatively easy to dog to care for and does not require specialized attention. The amount of coat care depends on whether you have a smooth-coated, broken-coated or rough-coated Russell. Smooth coats need no more than weekly grooming; the workload steps up with the other two coat types.

We are fortunate that the Russell is a healthy breed, with no exaggerations, and he has a good life expectancy. Most Russells live into their teens, and some even make it to their mid- to late teens. Before taking on a Russell, you need to make a commitment to care for him for the duration of his life.

Extra
considerations

Before starting the quest for your Russell Terrier, you need to narrow your choice so you know exactly what you are looking for.

Male or female?

It would be easy to make many generalizations about how males can be more of a handful where females are a little more compliant and better suited to first-time terrier owners. Or how males can be 'sparkier' in training and females perhaps more temperamental when it suits them. Or how one is more loving; the other more independent, and so on. But it really isn't that simple! Russells are individuals and don't fit easily into any categories, least of all those based on gender.

When considering the sex of a puppy, it is a matter of personal preference and seeing what would best fit in with your family dynamics. If you have a male dog already, it is likely that he will accept a female more readily than a feisty little upstart of a male who thinks he's the bees-knees! Dogs of the opposite sex generally get along without problems – though, again, there are exceptions.

Remember, too, that male dogs and female dogs can get along rather too well – so one or the other would have to be neutered, to avoid unwanted pregnancies. Other considerations are that a female, unless neutered, will come into season approximately every six months, during which time she would have to be kept away from other dogs and exercised on a lead.

Entire male dogs can be prone to roaming, inter-male competitive aggression, mounting and scent marking. In some cases, neutering can prevent such problems, but not always. Where the behavior is not hormone-related, or has become habitual, neutering will not reduce the unwanted behaviors.

More than one?

Many people decide to get a puppy – but then end up with two. Either they can't decide on a single pup when visiting the litter and so get two on impulse, or they think that a single dog will be lonely if left and so opt to get him company.

Russells make great single dogs, but they can get along with other canines and many live with a doggie pal or two with no problems at all. In fact, they can thrive on the canine stimulation and fun games that can be had with a four-legged friend.

However, getting two pups at the same time is not advisable. First, there is the practical issue of being

unable to give each pup the individual time and attention needed for training. The first few months of having a puppy or new dog are very time-consuming. The pup will need careful supervision to ensure he's not getting into any mischief and danger, and training is also labor-intensive. The pup will need to be taken outside frequently for toileting, and will need watching like a hawk to ensure he remains clean in the house. To supervise two pups – especially two as energetic as Russell Terriers – you need two pairs of eyes and four hands!

There is also the bonding issue to consider. Two pups are likely to bond closely with each other – but to the detriment of your relationship with them. Why listen to you when there's fun to be had with a fellow partner in crime?

If you want two dogs, the best advice is to get one dog first and wait until he's at least 12 months old, fully trained, socialized and bonded to you, before getting another and starting the process all over again.

An older dog?

It may suit your lifestyle to miss out on the puppy stage and take on an older dog. In some cases, a Parson Russell breeder may be willing to part with a youngster who has not fulfilled his early potential and is therefore not suitable for showing. It could be that a female has come to the end of her breeding career, or an older dog is to be retired from the show ring. In these situations, the breeder may consider that a dog will benefit from having one-on-one care and attention rather than living in a multi-dog household.

If you decide on an older Russell, you will need to be patient and help him settle into a new home, as it can be quite upsetting to change homes at this later stage.

Rescued dogs

There are many reasons why dogs end up in rescue centers and, often, it is through no fault of their own. It could be due to marriage break up, moving homes, changing jobs, or even a new addition to the human family. These dogs have done nothing wrong – they simply find themselves without a home. However, there are some cases where a Russell may be rehomed because his family cannot cope with his behavior. This nearly always happens when the dog has been bought on a whim, and no one has taken responsibility for training him.

If you think you can provide a loving, permanent home for a rescued dog, find out as much as possible about his history and background. It is essential that you know what you are taking on, and are confident that you will be able to cope. The worst scenario is to rehome a dog and then to hand him back a few weeks later. A dog that is put up for rescue has already been through a lot of trauma, so talk to the rehoming staff, and take your time before making a final decision.

Below: Can you provide a forever home for a rescued dog?

Sourcing a puppy

When you decide the time is right for taking on a puppy, the temptation is to buy from the first litter you track down. This would be a big mistake; you need to do your homework and spend time finding a breeder that produces dogs most likely to suit your needs.

The first consideration is whether you are opting for a Parson Russell, a working Jack Russell, or a pet Jack Russell. If you have your heart set on the show-type Parson Russell Terrier, the first port of call should be your national Kennel Club. Both the American Kennel Club (AKC) and the UK Kennel Club (KC) have excellent websites which provide a wealth of information about the breed.

You will also find a register of breeders who have puppies available. Both kennel clubs run schemes for breeders – the AKC breeders of merit, and the KC assured breeders – and if a breeder has signed up to these schemes it means they have adhered to an agreed code of practice. You can also contact the Parson Russell breed clubs; the secretaries will have lists of breeders with litters available in your area.

If it is more the working-type of Russell that appeals, you will need to contact the Jack Russell Terrier

Club of America, or the Jack Russell Terrier Club of Great Britain, to locate breeders.

If you want a short-legged pet type, then you can go to rescue shelters for an older dog or puppy. Jack Russells are numerous – and you are likely to find a litter in a rescue centre. Alternatively, ask your vet or dog training club if they know of a litter.

Buyer beware!

Regardless of the type of Russell you are looking for, caution must be observed to avoid puppy farmers, who churn out litter after litter of puppies of all breeds and types, with no regard for the pups or the parents.

Questions, questions, questions

When you have located a breeder, you need to ask many important questions to find out if the puppies are well bred and well reared; a reputable breeder will be only too pleased to provide you with as much information as you require. Ask the following:

- How many puppies are there in the litter?

- What is the make up of males and females?

- Where has the litter been reared? Ideally this will be in a home setting where the puppies will have had all the benefits of early socialization.

- Can I see the mother and any other close relatives? It is essential to see the mother interact with her puppies as this will give you some indication of the temperament they are likely to inherit. It will also help if you see close relatives so you get a feeling for the 'type' of dog the breeder produces.

- Can I see the father? This is unlikely as, often, the sire will not be living on the premises. However, you should be able to see a photo and a pedigree, plus his show record if applicable.

- Have the parents been health-tested? The fact that the Russell has been bred for function for so long has held the breed in good stead in terms of health.

However, there are some conditions, such as an eye condition known as primary lens luxation, which may occur in some lines. For more information, see page 187.

In turn, the breeder will ask you some searching questions which may include the following:

- What is your family set-up?

- Do you have experience with dogs, and with Russell Terriers in particular?

- Is there someone who will be at home to look after the puppy?

- Do you have a securely-fenced garden?

Do not take offence; the breeder needs to make sure you can provide a suitable home for one of their precious puppies. If a breeder does not ask questions, you should be very wary as they may be more interested in making a sale than caring about the welfare of the puppies.

Facing page:
The breeder will
need to find out if you
and your family are
suited to owning a
Russell Terrier.

Puppy watching

Puppies are irresistible – Russell puppies perhaps more so than most. But this is a time when you should try not to let your heart rule your head. Go and visit with an open mind, and only proceed if you are 100 per cent happy with everything you find.

The best age to view a litter of puppies is when they are around six weeks old. By this time, they are active and playful, and you will be able to get some idea of their individual personalities. Puppies do sleep a lot, so try to arrange your visit when they are most likely to be lively. The breeder will advise you on this.

Look out for the following signs of a healthy, well-reared litter:

- The environment where the puppies are being kept should be clean and smell fresh. There should be clean bedding, and a variety of toys for the puppies to play with.

- The puppies should be interested in everything that is going on, and be ready to come up and greet you.

- If they hear an unexpected, loud noise, it is natural for them to be startled. But watch how quickly they recover and go back to their games. This 'recovery time' will give you an indication of how well they will cope once they have left the safety of the nest.

- The puppies' eyes should be clear and bright with no sign of discharge or weeping. Any redness or irritation is a warning sign that something is wrong.

- Are the ears clean? The pups should not scratch persistently at their ears or shake their heads.

- Assess each puppy's size and shape. Does the pup look well fed? A slightly plump pup is fine, but beware a very round tummy, as this could indicate an unhealthy worm burden.

- Inspect the coat, stroking it in the wrong direction so you can see any signs of dandruff or parasites (either fleas or mites, or the brown specks of their dirt). Part the coat and inspect the skin to ensure it is healthy.

- Lift the pup's tail. The anus and surrounding area should be clean, with no feces or soreness.

- Watch the pup move. His actions should be free, with no signs of limping, restricted movement, or pain.

Picking a puppy

If you are looking for a family pet, it is best to ask the breeder, who has spent many hours watching the puppies, to help you make your choice. For novice dog owners, it is generally advised that the boldest pup is avoided, as he is more likely to need a confident, dog-savvy owner. Such a dog could be ideal for agility, heelwork to music or obedience, but would run rings around an inexperienced owner or in a home with limited opportunities for learning. The shyest pup is also better suited to an experienced handler, as he will need confident handling and socialization.

If you are planning to get involved with showing, you will need to look at the puppies more closely to see which has the most potential. Again, the breeder will help you with this, putting each puppy in a show pose so you can see how closely he adheres to the Breed Standard. Ideally, invite someone who is experienced in showing Parson Russells to view the litter with you.

A Russell Terrier friendly home

You need to plan ahead before you collect your pup, so you have all the equipment, food and toys ready for your new arrival. You will also need to make sure your home and garden are free from potential hazards. These preparations apply to a new puppy but, in reality they are the means of creating an environment that is safe and secure for your Russell Terrier throughout his life.

In the home

Unless you have recently had small children in the family, you are probably oblivious to the hidden dangers in your home. Toddlers, like puppies, seem drawn to danger – they seem to seek it out wherever they are!

It is important to get a pup's perspective on your home. For this, divest your dignity and get on all fours. Start in one room, and work your way around your home; you will be amazed at the troublespots you find – electric cables, the bowl of tempting fruit on the coffee table, the poinsettia (which is toxic to dogs) on the windowsill that can be reached by climbing on the sofa, the shoes by the back door, the designer handbag by the armchair... the list is endless.

The best advice is to limit your pup to a few rooms in the house – say, the kitchen and the lounge – that you can fully puppy-proof. Use a stairgate to restrict access elsewhere and a puppy crate for when you cannot supervise your Russell.

Make sure that the cupboards in the kitchen have child-proof locks, so your pup cannot eat what he shouldn't, and keep all chemicals (such as household bleach) in cupboards that are out-of-reach of your Russell.

In the garden

Below: Look at your home from a puppy's viewpoint.

First, inspect your boundaries. A reputable breeder should have asked or checked about the suitability of your garden before allowing you to book a puppy. A reputable rescue organization will have done a home-check prior to allowing you to adopt a pup or adult Russell. But it's best to double-check.

It should come as no surprise to hear that Russells – like all terriers – love to dig, and they are very good at it. Even if your fences have no holes underneath them now, they will need checking daily once you bring your Russell home. Ideally, the fence will be sunk into the ground at least six inches (15 cm) – more if you have a champion digger. You will also need to make sure that gates have secure fastenings, and family members are drilled to keep them closed.

Bear in mind that your Russell is also likely to dig up your prize plants and shrubs, so if there is an area of the garden that you would like to preserve from possible devastation, fence it off. In your dog's part of the garden, provide him with an area where he is allowed to dig. That way, he can fulfill his natural instincts – without you getting upset. Either dig over a section of the garden and hide some of his toys in it, or provide him with his own doggie sandpit.

In the garage and shed, make sure that all hazards, such as saws, shears, petrol, pesticides, and anti-freeze, are out of reach. Similarly, when using any product in the garden, make sure you use only those tested as pet-safe, and follow the instructions carefully – keeping your dog away from any treated areas for the time specified.

Buying equipment

There is some basic equipment you will need to buy before you collect your puppy. It is advisable to go for good quality gear, which should, with luck, last you for many years to come.

Indoor crate

This should be considered an essential purchase as it is a means of keeping your puppy safe at times when you cannot supervise him, and it will protect your home from his destructive tendencies.

Some owners worry that an indoor crate is like a cage, but this is not how a Russell views it. He sees his crate as a cosy den, where he can rest in peace. In fact, many Russells opt to use their crates in adulthood so it is worth buying a crate that will accommodate a fully grown dog.

As Russell Terriers vary in size, it is not possible to give precise measurements, but you will need a crate that is big enough to allow your Russell to stand up, turn around and stretch out.

Bedding

The crate will need to be lined with bedding. The best type to buy is synthetic fleece, which is absorbent, allowing moisture to soak through in case of accidents. It is easy to wash and dry, and is fairly indestructible. You will need a minimum of two pieces, so you can rotate them when one needs washing.

To begin with a puppy cannot last through the night without needing to relieve himself. For this reason, it is a good idea to put newspaper at the front of the crate. A puppy will try not to soil his bedding, and so he will use the newspaper, which will make cleaning up much easier.

Below: Delay buying a bed until your Russell has got through the chewing stage.

Dog bed

There is a dog bed for every taste and budget. There is a booming market in novelty dog beds, shaped like racing cars or castles, and you can even buy handcrafted, four-posted dog beds! This may tickle the owner's fancy, but, to honest, your Russell pup will be just as comfortable, possibly more so, in a bed fashioned from a cardboard box and lined with cosy, fleecy veterinary-type bedding. Just remove any staples from the box, remove the top, and cut the sides down a bit. Then, if your Russell does take to chewing his bed – as most do when young – you simply replace with a new box. Once your pup has outgrown the chewing phase, you can then invest in something more permanent. Most Russell owners opt for a plastic bed, lined with bedding. This is comfortable, easy to clean, and virtually indestructible.

Bowls

At least two bowls are needed – one for food and one for water. Stainless-steel bowls are the best choice – as they will last forever, cannot be broken, and are lightweight, hygienic and easy to clean. A travel bowl will also be useful for walks and for in the car. They come in a range of materials and styles – from fold-up material ones, to plastic ones with an inbuilt water reserve, or water bottles with a pullout bowl attachment.

Food

The best advice is to stick to the food recommended by your puppy's breeder while he settles in his new home. Breeders provide some food in their puppy packs, but it is a good idea to stock up before you collect the pup. Make sure you ask the breeder in advance what food the Russell is used to, so you can make the necessary preparations.

For more information on feeding, see page 100.

Collar and lead

When choosing a collar and lead, don't just be governed by how cute your puppy looks! There are some brilliant designs available, but make sure they are practical and comfortable, both for the dog and the holder of the lead – you! A soft, adjustable collar and a lightweight lead will help with early training, as your puppy will scarcely notice them.

While you are in the pet shop, make sure you get an identification tag. These can either be ordered in the store, or some have machines that do them on the spot for you.

Grooming gear

You will need the following items:

- A small puppy toothbrush and dog toothpaste

- A mild puppy shampoo

- A slicker brush

- Narrow-toothed comb

- A stripping knife (if you have a rough or broken-haired dog and wish to hand strip him yourself)

- Guillotine-type nail clippers.

Toys

Russells are such playful dogs, they will find a game with any object! Unfortunately, these can include items that you treasure, so make sure you give your terrier some toys of his own to play with.

In common with most terriers, Russells love squeaky toys – biting them, shaking them and delighting in 'killing' their small prey. However, they should only be used for occasional play, not only because the noise will drive you to distraction, but because a Russell can bite through the toy, loosen the plastic 'squeak' and swallow it. To save veterinary emergencies, this is a toy for supervised play only.

Russells can enjoy tug toys, too, but they should only be used for play between dogs, or for gentle, occasional play with people. Vigorous pulling on the tug can cause dental damage.

Russells can also become quite competitive about winning tug games, so make sure you 'win' more games than you 'lose', and also train him to 'leave' on command, so you stay in control of the toy.

A Kong is a must-have for all dogs. They are virtually indestructible, rubber, cone-shaped toys in which treats can be stuffed. A dog will amuse himself for ages, trying to get the food out; they are therefore ideal for crate use when you need to leave your dog for an hour or so.

Finding a vet

If you are not already registered with a vet, you will need to find a practice before you collect your puppy. The best starting point is word-of-mouth recommendation from dog-owning friends in your area. Once you have some names, contact the surgeries and ask if you can pay a visit. You need to find out what facilities are available, if the staff have experience with Russell Terriers, and what provision is made for emergency cover.

Settling in

At last the time has come to collect your puppy. This is the day you and your family have been waiting for, but you need to remember it is something of an ordeal for a puppy. Even the boldest Russell pup can feel overwhelmed as he makes the transition to his new home.

When you arrive home, take the pup out to your garden, to an area that you have allocated for toileting purposes. When he has had a little sniff around and investigated every nook and cranny, he could well toilet. If he does so, praise him and give him a treat. If he is always taken to this spot to toilet, it will help to build an association in his mind.

Next, take him inside, to your puppy-proofed home and let him explore the rooms he is allowed access to. Don't overwhelm him; allow him to explore, and give him lots of reassurance if he appears worried.

Puppies, like babies, need plenty of sleep and tire easily, so putting him in his crate for a half-hour nap

would be a good idea. Make sure it is cosy, with soft bedding, a blanket draped over the top, to make it den-like, and in a quiet, draught-free corner. Put a stuffed puppy Kong in with him, and perhaps a towel or blanket that has come from the breeder, to give him a reassuring, familiar scent.

The resident dog

If you already have a dog at home, you need to ensure relations get off to a good start. Introduce the two of them in the garden, which is relatively neutral territory. Ideally, your resident dog should be off-lead – unless he is very boisterous – as he will be able to behave more naturally, allowing the puppy to pick up all-important signals and body language.

If the puppy is a bit pushy and the older dog gives a warning growl, do not interfere. The puppy needs to learn to mind his manners, and he will understand that he needs to show a little more respect. It is far better to allow the two dogs to work out their own relationship with a minimum of human interference.

Make sure you do not make your resident dog feel jealous by lavishing too much attention on the puppy. Spend some quality time with him – this is easy to do when you are out on walks without the puppy – so that he knows he is still very special.

No matter how well the two dogs appear to be getting on, do not leave them on their own together when you go out, unless the puppy is in a crate. A situation could flare up when you are not there to supervise, and it is always better to be safe than sorry.

Meeting the family

If you have children in the family, try to keep proceedings as calm as possible. Ask the children to sit on the floor, and give each of them a treat for the dog. Allow the puppy to go up to each child, and he can be given a stroke and a treat. You can introduce some toys and the children can play with him, making sure the game does not get too rough. Remember, high-pitched voices and waving arms are highly stimulating, and a puppy will become over-excited, and may even nip, if you allow this sort of behavior.

It is also important that all members of the family know what is allowed – and what is not allowed – with regard to the puppy. For example, is he allowed on the sofa, or to go upstairs? Is he allowed to jump up, or to run off with a toy when he is playing? These are decisions you need to make, and then you must be 100 percent consistent so your puppy understands what is required of him.

After a day or two of settling in, once the pup knows who his family is, friends can start visiting – they won't need to be asked twice!

Facing page: Take care with initial interactions and your Russell will become an outstanding family companion.

Introducing house pets

A Russell Terrier will naturally hunt cats, and some will kill them if given a chance. But that is not to say that a Russell cannot live happily with a feline in the family if he is raised with the cat from puppyhood. Introductions should be very carefully supervised. Never leave the pair alone unsupervised until they have both demonstrated repeated indifference to each other. You cannot be too careful.

Fit stairgates, so the cat can be left in peace upstairs (make sure you move the littertray, bed and food/water bowls) and can choose when he wants to come down. A couple of times a day, put the pup in his crate and encourage puss to spend time in the same room as the crated pup. With the pup contained safely, the curious cat will be able to assess him without the chance of being chased. Once they get used to the sight, scent and sound of each other, the novelty will have worn off when they actually meet without bars between them.

When the first non-crate meetings occur, keep your puppy on a lead, and reward and praise quietly when he looks at you and doesn't take notice of the cat. It is very important that your puppy never has an opportunity to chase – if he does, puss will run and pup will think it a great game.

Once they get to the relaxed stage of really not taking much notice of each other, non-lead encounters can take place, but do make sure that puss has access to high-up safe places (a secure bookshelf or high windowsill) where he can take refuge if necessary.

With other pets, such as hamsters, gerbils and rabbits, do not even try to create household harmony. Keep them securely out of your Russell's reach – or there will be tears all round.

The first night

There are various schools of thought as to the best way of getting through the first few nights with your pup. One advocates putting the pup in his crate at bedtime and not going to him until he is released in the morning – regardless of how he howls.

Within a night or two he realizes that his cries are in vain, so he shuts up. Going to the pup each time he cries, they say, only teaches him that if he yells, someone comes running – and so he will never learn to go through the night on his own.

The other camp takes a kinder approach. They recognise that it is only natural for a pup to howl at night when he is in his new home. He is away from his mother and littermates for the first time in his life, and he is in a new home with new people. No wonder he feels a little insecure.

Some people advise going to the pup each time he cries, reassuring him and settling him back to sleep. Others advise putting the crate in your bedroom for the first week or so, so he doesn't feel alone. Once he is used to his new environment, then the crate can be moved.

Personally, I do the latter. If a pup howls or cries in the crate in your bedroom, you can just quietly speak to him to reassure him you are nearby. You will be in for a few broken nights, but this phase doesn't last long – provided you don't succumb and let him sleep in the bed with you.

It is inevitable that your puppy will miss his littermates to begin with.

House training

House training is usually the part of puppy ownership that first-time owners dread – but it is actually very simple provided you follow some basic rules.

Pups come pre-programmed to be clean in the house. From when they are tiny, in the nest with their littermates, they will move away from where they sleep and eat in order to relieve themselves. The key to successful house training a pup in his new home is to teach him that the entire house is his den, and that he should defecate outside.

First allocate an area of the garden to be used for toileting. Take your puppy to this spot regularly – every hour when he's eight weeks old – plus at other key times when pups are more likely to need to relieve themselves:

- When he first wakes up

- After a meal

- After a nap

- After a period of excitement (such as meeting new people, playing, training and so on).

It is also important to be vigilant throughout the day and to take your pup outside if he exhibits any sign of needing to relieve himself. He might start to circle, sniff the ground, seek out a quiet corner, behind furniture, or actually squat. Immediately run to the outside door, calling him in a happy, excited tone of voice so he will follow you. Then lead him to his toileting spot and praise him to the skies when he 'performs' there.

When you take your pup outside, do not engage with him. Let him have a sniff around and, when he eventually relieves himself, say the verbal cue you have chosen, e.g. "Get busy", and then praise him and give him a treat. Even if it is cold, dark or wet, do not immediately rush inside after your puppy has performed. Instead, stay outside for a few minutes and have a game with him, so he does not start to adopt delaying tactics to prolong his time in the garden. With repetition, he will learn to associate the verbal cue with the action of relieving himself and will eventually perform when asked.

When accidents happen

Below: *Vigilance is the key to successful house training.*

If your puppy has an accident in the house, do not react negatively. If you shout at him, he will not understand why you are being so mean – and it will only serve to harm your relationship with him. Worse, he might associate toileting with your anger and so will avoid doing it in front of you again – even when he is outside. If you want to shout at anyone, shout at yourself for not being sufficiently attentive.

If your puppy does have an accident, clean it up promptly using a non-ammonia cleaner. Proprietary cleaners are available for this purpose. Using a cleaner with ammonia could well attract the puppy back to the spot again, as it will smell of urine to him.

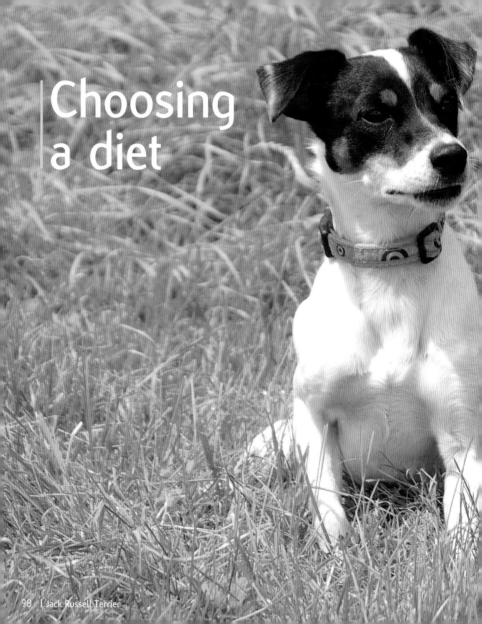

Choosing
a diet

There are so many different types of diet to choose from, it is easy to feel overwhelmed if you are new to dog ownership. The aim is to find a diet that is suited to your individual dog, and one that is convenient for you to feed.

When a puppy first arrives in his new home, it is suggested that you feed the diet recommended by his breeder for the few weeks. If it seems to suit your Russell, there is no reason to change.

However, you may have problems getting hold of the brand, or your puppy may not be thriving on it, in which case, you will want to investigate other options.

If you go down this route, remember to make the changeover as gradual as possible, to avoid stomach upsets. Replace a little of the usual food with his new food, and, over the course of about 10 days, increase the ratio of new food to old until a complete change has been completed.

When choosing a diet, you need to examine the pros and cons of each method of feeding:

Natural diets

Many people advocate feeding fresh food to dogs. There are various diets to choose from, including two from vets: Dr Ian Billinghurst's Barf diet, which stands for biologically appropriate raw food (often best known as bones and raw food), and Tom Lonsdale's Raw Meaty Bones diet.

If you would like to feed naturally, research the diet well, as nutritional deficiencies can be harmful. The Barf diet is covered in Dr Billinghurst's book Give A Dog A Bone, and Tom Lonsdale has written Work Wonders, both of which explain their diets to the novice. There are also plenty of websites and chatrooms dedicated to natural feeding, which are easily found through a reputable search engine.

If you make adaptations to the Billinghurst or Lonsdale diet, do ask your vet for advice, to ensure your dog's nutritional needs are being met, or ask to be referred to a veterinary nutritionist. Be aware of the dangers of feeding bones to dogs. The advocates for natural diets say they are minimal, and that the benefits of natural feeding more than compensate for the risk, but it is important to assess the risk yourself.

Preparing a natural diet can be time-consuming, but there is a middle way. Dr Billinghurst, for example, has a range of Barf foods that you can buy, and other manufacturers also produce natural foods. Ask at your pet store or search online for local suppliers.

Commercial diets

The pet food industry is big, big business, with a range to suit every type of dog, budget and taste.

Dogs generally love wet food, which comes in tins or pouches – it is smelly and rich and is usually wolfed down quickly. Usually fed with biscuits, it can be too rich for some, producing soft stools in some dogs, and it goes off quickly once opened. It is a popular choice with people whose dogs are fussy eaters and who turn up their noses at dried complete diets.

Dried, complete diets are very popular with owners and are a safe bet. They provide all the nutrients a dog needs, and are very convenient: they are easy to feed, clean, and easy to store. Complete diets do your thinking for you, and are usually available in life stages – from puppy to adult and on to senior – addressing a dog's nutritional needs as he matures.

One word of warning: when researching what food to give your Russell, do check the 'nutritional analysis' label on the side of the packet. Like most terriers, Russells can be hyperactive and some react badly to additives – particularly artificial colorings and flavourings. If your Russell becomes more manic

You need to find a diet that suits your Russell's age and lifestyle.

than usual on a particular type of food, switch to a more natural alternative, and perhaps one that is lower in protein. If a change of diet doesn't help, seek the advice of your vet, who can investigate any medical causes for the behavior and refer you to a behaviorist if necessary.

Number of meals

Being a smaller dog, it is preferable to feed a Russell two small meals a day as an adult, as opposed to one large one. This helps to give him a continuous supply of energy throughout the day, rather than all in one hit, keeping his blood sugars more stable.

Puppies need feeding more frequently and your breeder should provide you with a diet sheet when you collected your Russell. As a guide, an eight-week-old puppy is fed four times a day, with one meal being dropped by around 16 weeks of age. By six months of age the pup is usually down to two meals a day.

With an old dog, a vet may recommend three small meals a day. Older Russells may lose interest if faced with a large meal – offering small amounts more frequently throughout the day can help to keep up their energy.

Ideal weight

Below: Monitor the amount you feed as your puppy grows.

The weight of a Russell entirely depends on his build and type. A pedigree Parson Russell Terrier weighs anything from 13 lb to 17 lb (6-8 kg). Working terriers are traditionally 1 lb an inch, so around 14 lb (6.5 kg) for a 14-inch (35-cm) dog in good condition. Heavier-boned dogs can be another pound or two on top. The short-legged pet-type Russell varies from the miniature to the giant, so weight can be anything from 9 lb (4 kg) upwards.

Your dog's ideal weight will depend on his type and stature. You should be able to see his ribs, but they should not be prominent. His body, when viewed from above, should have shape (not a brick shape!) and a waist should be visible.

Do not underestimate the dangers of obesity. It is not purely an aesthetic issue: there are many health dangers, including heart problems, mobility, and diabetes.

Of course, if your dog suddenly puts on weight or loses weight, seek veterinary advice.

Bones and chews

It is important to provide your dog with safe chews throughout his life. Puppies need to gnaw in order to alleviate the pain of teething when they lose their milk teeth. But, even in adulthood, dogs derive great pleasure from chewing.

Finding a safe chew or bone is vitally important. A rubber Kong, stuffed with some Kong filler pate, peanut butter, some canned food, dry kibble, and/or cheese will keep a Russell amused.

Nylon-type bones are popular too, or sterilised bones from the pet store. Never give your dog a cooked bone; it will splinter and produce sharp fragments, which, when swallowed, could have very serious repercussions.

Water

Always ensure that your dog has access to fresh water. This is especially important if you feed a dry diet and do not pre-soak it. If you do soak your dog's dry food, you will know how much moisture it absorbs – think about what this would do inside your dog's tum if he doesn't have enough to drink!

Right: Gnawing on a chew will promote dental health.

Caring for your Russell Terrier

The Russell Terrier is a relatively easy breed to care for, but like all animals, he has his own special needs which you must take on board in order to keep him happy and healthy.

Grooming

If you have a pedigree Parson Russell Terrier, the breeder may have included details of how to groom him in the puppy pack you were given on purchase. Some breeders also encourage their buyers to bring their dogs back for grooming lessons when the adult coat has come through. Alternatively, you can ask breeders at shows (once they have finished competing) for advice or contact a breed club for details.

Grooming a Russell of any type is not difficult. These

are hardy, low-maintenance dogs whose coats were their protective jackets against any briars or weather they encountered. Smooth-coated Russells really need very little – just a brush through the coat with a slicker brush once a week to remove loose hair. When the coat is shed in the Spring, daily brushing is advisable. Finish by going through the coat with a narrow-toothed comb to catch any stray loose hairs.

Rough- or broken- coated Russells need to be hand-stripped, where the dead hairs are plucked out. It can be a time-consuming task, but, with practice, you and your terrier will soon get used to it, and it only needs doing once or twice a year in pet dogs. Show dogs will need more frequent attention to keep the coat looking tip-top.

It is advisable to get your Russell puppy used to being groomed and handled from the age of eight weeks. If he associates grooming with a relaxing experience that is handsomely rewarded

The workload increases if you own a broken or rough-coated Russell.

afterwards, he is more likely to grow up a willing participant.

Stripping

First, make sure the coat is ready for stripping. It should already have started to shed. Test the coat by gripping some hair between your finger and thumb (or use a stripping knife if you prefer – many people find it helps to give a better grip). If it is difficult to pull, leave the hair for a week or two before trying again.

- When the coat is ready, brush thoroughly with a slicker brush – first against the natural direction of the coat, and then the other way. This will help to dislodge loose hairs.

- Now do the same with a comb, then dust some chalk into the coat so it will be easier to grip the hair.

- Comb the hair upwards, grasp the hair between your finger and thumb, and pull in the direction that the hair naturally lies. Everyone has their own system as to where they start and finish. For example, you might want to start at the chest, work along the back and sides, and then do the underside, legs and finally the face. After a couple of strips you will no doubt have devised your own 'route'.

Prior to stripping, go through the coat with a slicker brush.

To strip the coat, grasp the hair between finger and thumb and pull gently.

The head will need attention.

Work you way along the body to the hindquarters, not forgetting the tail.

- For the face, use a smaller slicker brush and then pluck the hair on the muzzle and under the eyes, before turning your attention to the neck.

- Strip the legs (including elbows and knees) and the feet, and finish by trimming around the feet with scissors, to create a neat outline.

- For the tummy, pluck the long hairs to create a smooth line. In male Russells, very carefully trim the hair around the penis.

- When you have finished stripping, brush the coat all over once more and then stand back to assess your dog and look at his outline, removing any stray hairs you may have missed.

After a couple of months, there will be further hair shedding, as the new coat grows through. Daily brushing will help to collect any loose hair – and save your vacuum cleaner from working overtime.

Some people find that stripping is a chore and prefer to clip the coat instead. It is certainly cheaper to get a groomer to clip the coat than to strip it (and cheaper still to buy your own clippers and do it yourself). There is a lot less work involved, but the coat texture will be softer. Show dogs should never be clipped, as the coat will be ruined in terms of the correct, harsh coat required in the Breed Standard.

Some groomers use thinning scissors to get rid of the dead hair.

The legs can be tidied with scissors.

The feet should look neat and cat-like.

Trim the underside for a clean outline.

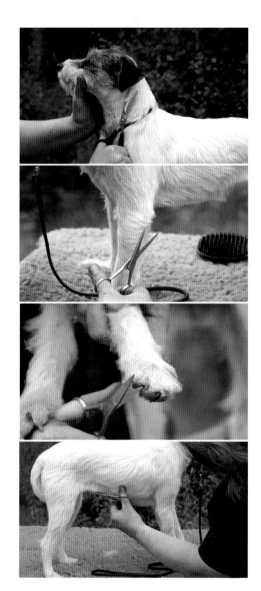

Bathing

The Russell's coat is made of stern stuff! Even if your terrier gets covered from nose to paw in mud, you will be amazed at how the dirt just falls off when it dries, and, with a quick brush, the coat is left looking like new underneath. Exhibitors often swear that over-bathing softens the coat and so bath their dogs minimally. However, pet dogs will usually need one or two baths a year to keep them smelling sweet – especially if they have rolled in something foul!

Regular checks

Once a week set aside a few minutes to give your dog the once-over. Brush him and run your hands over his body, inspecting him for any lumps, abrasions, parasites etc. If you spot anything of concern, ask your vet for advice; it is easier to deal with problems at the earliest opportunity.

Teeth

Get your Russell puppy used to having his teeth brushed so that he accepts the attention when he is older and has his permanent, adult teeth.

- First, stroke around the muzzle, progressing to lifting the lips to check your Russell's teeth. Speak soothingly, and reward when the pup is calm and relaxed.

Even in the show ring, the Russell should always retain the appearance of a working dog.

- Progress to rubbing the teeth, either with a rubber fingerbrush over the end of your finger or a piece of muslin.

- Some doggie toothpaste (available from pet stores) will be a welcome reward – it comes in lots of meaty flavours, which dogs love.

Brushing daily is ideal, which, with the occasional dental chew thrown in, will help to keep your dog's breath fresh and his teeth sparkling clean. Many dogs need expensive dental treatment by middle-age, which necessitates an anesthetic, and this can be avoided with regular brushing throughout your Russell's life.

Ears

Russells investigate everything head-first – so they are prone to getting seeds and other undergrowth and debris stuck to their faces and inside their ears. Once a week, check your dog's ears – as well as after an adventurous walk. If the ears look red, smell, or your dog is shaking his head and/or pawing at his ear, take him to the vet. He could have ear mites, which are easily treatable with a cleaner/ear drops, or he could have a grass seed that has burrowed down into the ear canal and needs careful removal.

Nails

If you can hear your dog clip-clopping as he walks across a wooden floor, his nails are too long. Many dogs rarely need their nails cut, as they naturally wear them down when exercising on hard surfaces, but dogs that are mostly exercised on soft ground, or dogs with poor foot conformation, may need a helping hand to keep their nails trim.

Russells usually have white nails, which takes some of the tension out of clipping, as it is easy to see the dark 'quick' inside the nail. This 'quick' is the blood supply; if nicked, it will bleed and will be painful for your dog –
something he will

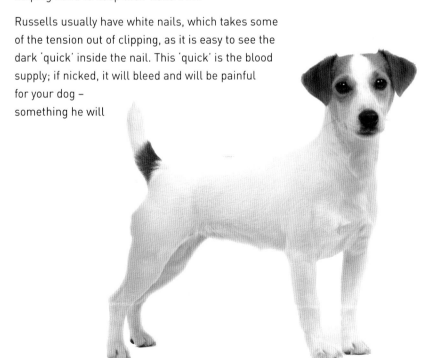

remember every time you bring out the nail clippers in future!

The best advice is to clip off just a small bit at a time and always to err on the side of caution. If your Russell has dark nails be particularly careful. Using guillotine-type clippers is easier than conventional clippers, as you can see precisely what is being cut, and it is advisable to have a styptic pen to hand, which will stop the bleeding if you do have an accident.

For the first clip, it is a good idea to ask your vet or a groomer to give you a demonstration.

Exercising your Russell

The Russell is an active little fellow; he thrives in a busy family household where he can take part in all activities, but is equally happy as the sole companion of an older, active person who likes walking and pottering about in the garden. This is not a dog for the couch potato!

As a minimum, two half-hour walks of safe free-running will keep a fully grown adult sane, together with play in the garden and a busy daytime schedule (accompanying you on errands and the like). Most Russells will happily walk for miles and love to explore new places. Do ensure that your Russell's recall is reliable, of course, as terriers are known for their selective deafness.

Puppies do not need lots of exercise – indeed, it can be detrimental if they have too much while they are still growing and their skeletons are forming. Play in the garden, and, when they are protected by their vaccinations, short lead walks for socialization purposes, will suffice.

The older Russell

Russells age well. They are small, hardy dogs and remain active well into old age. They certainly stay playful all their lives – many would say that a Russell never grows up!

However, it is important to be aware a dog's needs do change as he grows older. Despite his determination to keep going, he will slow up and it may be better to take him for a couple of shorter walks rather than a lengthy hike. Your Russell's diet may also need adjusting – perhaps switch to the senior version of his dry complete diet, if this is what he's given, or reduce the size of his meals to account for his reduced activity.

Keep up with your dog's annual veterinary check-ups and seek advice between appointments if you are concerned about his health. Veterinary medicine is an exciting world, with new treatments being developed all the time.

The sooner any problem is noticed and reported, the sooner it can be addressed.

The same applies to character changes. If your Russell becomes grumpier, for example, it could well be because he is in pain. If he is drinking or eating more or less, you should also report to your vet.

Below: Be aware of the changing needs of your Russell Terrier.

Letting go

Invincible as he may seem, the time will come when it is time to say goodbye to your Russell. Whether he dies peacefully in his sleep or is euthanised, the grief will be just the same. Russells are big, big characters and the hole they leave in our hearts is equally large.

Most pets are put to sleep, and it is a decision that no one likes to make. But it is your responsibility as your dog's carer to do your best by him. If he is suffering and there is no hope of recovery, it is your duty to ensure he keeps his dignity and is spared further pain.

Euthanasia can be performed at the surgery, or you can request a home visit, so your dog dies in the familiar surroundings of his home with his loved ones.

The sense of loss can be overwhelming and is nothing to be ashamed of. There are pet bereavement support services which can help you if you need someone to talk to. The pain may seem all-consuming immediately after your Russell's death, but it does ease with time. Eventually the tears will be replaced with smiles as you recall the good times you shared in your life together.

Social skills

When puppies are born, they are like a blank sheet of paper. It's the job of the breeder – and, after eight weeks, the new owner – to ensure that as many positive experiences are 'written' on the page as possible, in order that the Russell will be confident when he experiences similar or new things as an adult.

For this reason, it is crucial that puppies are reared in a home – and the busier the home, the better. If your Russell grows up in a happy, loving home, with children, cats, other dogs, and so on, where people are always coming and going, it will hold him in good stead for the future. In a quiet outbuilding, he won't get accustomed to ordinary family life, and all the usual noises that go with it, such as the vacuum cleaner, washing machine, food processor and saucepans accidentally being dropped.

So, at eight weeks, it's time to take the baton from the breeder and continue with your Russell's socialization programme...

The right start

The major socialization period for puppies is up to 12-14 weeks of age, so make the most of this window of opportunity. Unfortunately, this period coincides with the time when you need to physically protect him from contagious diseases. You therefore need to proceed with caution, avoiding places that are frequented by other dogs, and only allow your puppy to meet dogs that have been vaccinated. It's a case of making a risk assessment until your pup's second vaccinations offer him protection.

As a Russell puppy is small, you can carry him around in public places to begin with so he has the chance to become familiar with the outside world. Visit as many different people as you can, and, of course, ask your vet about puppy parties, where your Russell can be socialized with other pups. Do ensure that the party is supervised by someone with a good knowledge of dog behavior – a free-for-all where pups may be intimidated or bullied will do more harm than good.

The next stage

Once your pup's second vaccinations are effective (usually a week after the second jabs, but be guided by your vet), then socialization can steam ahead, with your pup meeting friendly older dogs, and as many different people as possible – young and old, male and female, from all different cultures and wearing as varied a wardrobe as possible. He can encounter all sorts of other animals (safely, on a lead), and different environments (busy train and bus stations, shopping areas, supermarket car parks and shops where dogs are permitted).

It is said that a puppy should meet at least 100 people by the time he is 12 weeks old – and these experiences should be positive, with the pup associating the people with happy, rewarding things. Get them to stroke him, play with him, give him a treat – and watch your pup's body language to ensure he's not intimidated or overwhelmed.

If a pup is worried by something, such as a loud noise, it is important not to react. Behave as if nothing has happened – ignore the loud noise and carry on as usual. Your pup will take his lead from you. If you are unworried, then he will think there is no cause for alarm.

With good socialization, a Russell will be calm and confident in all situations.

Training guidelines

When it comes to learning training exercises, the Russell is one smart cookie. Quick to learn, he can pick up new commands with ease, but this is only half the story. After all, he's a terrier – and, like many terriers, can be obstinate and 'deaf' at will!

The key is to motivate your dog to want to work with you. If training is a fun, enjoyable, rewarding game, your Russell will work his socks off. If he feels that it's boring and repetitive, he will be an unruly pupil.

Follow these guidelines to give you and your Russell the best chance of success:

- Find a reward your Russell Terrier really wants. This could be a toy or food, depending on the individual.

- If you are using food, vary the reward so you have high value treats (cheese or sausage) for teaching new exercises and recalls away from home, and low value treats (dry kibble) for routine training.

- If you are using a toy as a reward, make sure you only bring it out for training sessions so it has added value.

- Work on your tone of voice. This will be far more meaningful to your Russell Terrier than the words you are saying. Use a bright, happy, upbeat tone when you are training, and a deep, firm voice when you catch him red handed – raiding the bin, for example. Go over the top when you are praising your Russell so that he understands how pleased you are with him.

- Train in short sessions. This applies particularly to puppies which have a very short attention span. Adults will also switch off if sessions are too long.

- Never train if you are preoccupied or if you are in a bad mood. Your Russell will pick up on your negative vibes, and the session is doomed to failure.

- Teach one lesson at a time and only proceed to the next lesson when the first has been mastered.

- Praise success lavishly and ignore failure. You do not have to tell your dog off if he gets it wrong. Simply ignore what he has done, use a bright, positive tone of voice and tell him to "Try again".

- If your Russell is struggling with an exercise, break it down into stages so you can reward him at every step, and he has a clearer understanding of what is required.

- Make sure training sessions always end on a positive note – even if this means abandoning an exercise for the time being and finishing with something you know your Russell can do.

- Above all, make sure your training sessions are fun, with lots of play and plenty of opportunities to reward you dog, so that you both enjoy spending time together.

First lessons

It's never too soon to get started, so once your Russell has settled in his new home, you can start work on some mini training sessions. Remember, little and often is the golden rule at this early stage.

Wearing a collar

At first, use a light collar (such as nylon webbing) so your Russell gets used to the sensation of having something around his neck. Put it on your pup, making sure it is snug but not too tight. You should be able to get two fingers comfortably under the collar, but it shouldn't be so loose that it can come over his head.

When you put on the collar, distract your puppy with a game – if he's having fun, he will forget he is wearing a collar! After five or ten minutes, when he is distracted, remove the collar – don't remove it when he is scratching at it, or he will learn that this action results in the collar disappearing. Over time, gradually increase the length of time he wears a collar.

You can begin training as soon as you bring home your puppy.

Don't forget to check the fit of the collar regularly. Pups grow quickly and the collar will need replacing.

Lead-training

Once your Russell is used to wearing a collar, attach a light lead to it and just follow him around, ensuring the lead is slack. If there is any tension in the lead, he is likely to resist it and will do his finest impression of a mad kangaroo – leaping on the end of the lead, desperate to escape!

It is best to work on this aspect of training step by step:

- Say your pup's name, show him a treat, and, when you have his attention, take a couple of steps forward, encouraging him to walk alongside you. Reward any forward action on your pup's part and give lots of praise.

- Practise this for a few minutes only, but try to do it several times through the day.

- When your Russell does walk level with you, not pulling ahead or dragging behind, say "Heel" so he associates walking well with this cue word.

- If your dog pulls ahead of you, simply stop. He's pulling because he wants to get somewhere fast, so stop, call him back to your side, and calmly start again. Stop every time he pulls forward, and he will quickly realize that pulling is not a strategy that works.

Below: Remember your puppy only has a short attention span.

- When you start walking again, praise him immediately when he is in the correct position, and give him a treat, to reinforce that this behavior reaps rewards.

Come when called

The recall is the most important exercise you will ever teach your puppy and it can be a lifesaver in a number of situations. Even in everyday life, a good recall is a godsend – in the home and outside on walks. If a dog will not come reliably, he cannot be let off the lead safely and his exercise will be compromised.

The secret to a reliable recall is to start early when your puppy still naturally wants to follow you around the home. From the moment you bring your Russell home, start training; he will become more independent as he grows older and gains confidence, and will be less likely to co-operate.

- Start by calling your pup at mealtimes. As he approaches, have his food bowl at the ready, and he will get an instant reward. Remember, if a dog is rewarded for a behavior, he will repeat it.

- You can progress by increasing the distance, calling your pup when he is in the next room, and then presenting him with his food bowl.

- Make recall training fun by involving children or friends. Ask everyone to sit on the floor, and make sure they all have treats.

- One person gently restrains the pup and then, in turn, each person calls him, sounding bright and enthusiastic and using inviting body language – opening arms out wide to welcome the pup.

- The moment he is called, the pup is released, and as he reaches the person who is calling him, he is given a treat and lots of fuss. Keep practising and your Russell will quickly learn that "Come" is a fun game that always ends in a reward.

Gradually introduce more distractions as your puppy progresses with his training. Go out into the garden and when he is busy exploring, get his attention by calling his name and, asking him to "Come". When he responds, be ready with a treat – or a favorite toy – and give him lots of praise.

If he is slow to respond, try running away a few paces, or jumping up and down. It doesn't matter how silly you look, the key issue is to get your puppy's attention and then make yourself irresistible!

In a dog's mind, coming when called should be regarded as the best fun because he knows he is always going to be rewarded.

Never make the mistake of telling your dog off, no matter how slow he is to respond, as you will undo all your previous hard work.

Wait until you have built up a reliable recall at home before allowing your Russell to free run when you take him out. To start with, choose a safe area, with a minimum of distractions so you have the best chance of success.

Make sure you have a pocket full of treats, or a toy, so you can reward him at intervals throughout the walk when you call him to you.

Do not allow your Russell to free run and only call him back at the end of the walk to clip on his lead.

A dog as intelligent as a Russell will soon realize that the recall means the end of his walk and the end of fun – so who can blame him for not wanting to come back?

Stationary exercises

These basic training exercises are easy to teach, which will be rewarding for both you and your Russell. He will be starting to build up a repertoire of verbal cues he understands, and, if you give him a treat or a game with his toy when he responds correctly, he will be learning that it is worth his while to co-operate.

Sit

- Hold a tasty treat and show it to your puppy.

- When your Russell has had a sniff, he will follow it with his head, trying to get the tasty reward.

- Hold the treat above his head, to encourage him to look up, and then take it to just behind his nose, so he has to move his head backwards.

- The only way your pup can reach the treat is to put his bottom on the floor.

- The moment he does so, give him the treat and praise him to the skies.

- Once the penny has dropped, the pup will sit quicker – and you then reward only the promptest of responses.

- When the pup fully understands what is expected, say "Sit" as he sits, so he learns to associate the word with the action.

- With practice, he will sit on cue (when you ask) rather than you having to lure him into position with the treat.

Down

This is pretty simple once the dog has mastered the Sit, and is a very useful exercise. If your Russell will lie down on command, he cannot jump up at the postman, run out of an open door, chase the cat or get into any other mischief.

- Hold a tasty food reward in your palm, close your hand, with a little of the treat sticking out of your fist.

- Let your Russell have a sniff of your hand, so he realizes that there's something tasty inside, and then put your hand on the floor.

- Your Russell will try everything he can think of to

get the treat out of your hand. He will probably lean down on his front legs, trying to lick your hand; he might circle around you and see if he can get the treat if he approaches from a different direction... Eventually he will lie down. As soon as he does, give him the treat and lots of praise.

- The next time you do the exercise, the quicker he will realize what he has to do, and eventually he will lie down as soon as your closed fist hits the floor. At this point, introduce the word "Down" so he learns to associate the verbal cue with the action, and you can begin to withdraw the hand signal of the fist on the floor.

Right: The Down is one of the most useful exercises to teach.

Control exercises

When you have a dog as lively and as quick-witted as a Russell Terrier, it is vital to introduce a measure of control for his own safety as well as to instil good manners. Most Russells find these exercises quite taxing, as it is a struggle to inhibit their natural exuberance. However, patience and perseverance will pay off.

Wait

This exercise has a multitude of uses. Your Russell needs to learn to "Wait" when you open the car door so you can clip on his lead, when you open a door so he doesn't barge out first, and when you are ready to put his food bowl down. This exercise means " Wait" until I give the next command; the Stay exercise is used when you want your Russell to remain in position for an extended period.

- Ask your Russell to "Sit", and then stand and face him. It may be easier if he is on the lead to start with.

- Take one step back and hold up your hand, palm facing him, giving him a signal that effectively 'blocks' him.

- Pause for a few seconds, step back and reward with a treat.

- Keep practicing, gradually increasing the distance you can leave him.

- When you are confident that he understands what is required, introduce the verbal cue "Wait".

Stay

To differentiate this exercise from the "Wait", use a new hand signal.

- Start with your Russell in the Down, as he will be more secure in this position.

- Stand by his side and take a step forward, holding your arm behind you, with the palm of your hand facing him.

- Pause for a few seconds and then step back. Again, it may help if your Russell is on the lead in the early stages of training.

Gradually add distractions when you ask your Russell to "Stay".

- Keep practicing, extending the distance to the end of his lead before returning to his side. Give a release word, such as "OK", when the exercise is finished so that he knows he is free to break position.

- When your Russell fully understands what is required, introduce the verbal cue "Stay". Gradually build up the distance and the time you can leave your Russell.

Leave

This is another very useful command – for when your Russell spots a sandwich on the coffee table, or when you drop something that you don't want your terrier to run off with.

- First, give your Russell a treat. Then put another treat in your hand and close your fist around it.

- Put your fist in front of your dog. He will probably lick or nudge your hand, hoping to dislodge the treat, but ignore any such attempts. The moment your Russell takes his mouth away from your hand, open the fist so he can have the treat and give lots of praise.

- It won't take many practices before your clever terrier realizes that if he doesn't touch your hand, he gets a treat. At this stage you can introduce the verbal cue "Leave".

- Gradually build up the time that he will wait before being given the treat.

- Finally, move to putting the treat on the floor, rather than holding the reward.

Your Russell must learn to "leave" – even when he has something he values.

Opportunities for Russells

Russells are very adaptable little dogs, happy in many different types of home – from the active, retired couple to the young family. However, the successful owner knows that providing a loving home is not enough; a Russell needs opportunities to exercise his brain and body. There are many ways to keep your Russell occupied, with dog sports to suit everyone...

Good citizen scheme

The Good Citizen Scheme is run by the national Kennel Clubs in both the USA and the UK, and is designed to promote responsible ownership and to teach basic obedience and good manners so your dog is a model citizen in the community.   In the US there is one test; in the UK there are four award levels: Puppy Foundation, Bronze, Silver and Gold.

Obedience/Rally-O

Russells can do well in competitive obedience, though they can rarely achieve the precision given by the likes of the Border Collie. The independent Russell spirit can find the rigid training a bit stifling and repetitive – so do keep it fun!

Exercises include close heelwork, on and off the lead, sendaways, scent discrimination, distance control, recalls, retrieves, and stays. The exercises become harder the more the dog progresses through the levels and gains experience.

A growing offshoot of competitive obedience is rally-O, which is a very inclusive sport, open to dogs of all abilities. A mixture of obedience and agility, the dog and handler follow a course, which has 'stations' at various points, where specific exercises are asked for – such as a figure-of-eight, and a recall over a jump.

It's great fun and, since it is not quite as rigid in its need for perfect obedience (for example, a slightly crooked sit would not be penalized), it perhaps suits the Russell temperament more than competitive obedience.

Agility

This is great fun to watch and join in. Against the clock, at the fastest speed they can muster, dogs jump over obstacles, through tires and tunnels, and negotiate the contact equipment, which includes an A frame, a dog walk and a seesaw. Russells compete in classes for small dogs where the height of the jumps is lowered.

The Russell is quick to learn and can move at speed, and most do very well in this sport. The key is to find a focus, such as a favorite toy – preferably one he can 'kill' – so he is motivated to work for you.

Earthdog trials

The American Kennel Club run earthdog trials which are specifically designed to test the working ability of the small-legged terriers that were bred to "go to earth" in search of quarry. Man-made tunnels are created, and the dog must work the tunnels in order to find the quarry, which he will indicate by barking, scratching, or digging. The quarry (usually two rats) are protected by wooden bars across the end of the tunnel so they are not endangered.

To compete, Parson Russells must be registered with the AKC; the Jack Russell Terrier Club of America sanctions its own trials.

Flyball

This is another sport in which Russells can excel. It involves a straight run of 51 feet (15.5 metres), which has four small hurdles. At the end of the run is a flyball box, which, when triggered by the dog (with his paws), releases a tennis ball that the dog must catch.

He then returns with the ball, over the hurdles and back to the start/finish line. Once he crosses the line, the next dog in the team can start.

There are four dogs in each team, and two teams. The winning team is the one that finishes the course in the fastest time.

Heelwork to music/freestyle

This is where a dog and handler 'dance' to music. Heelwork to music is just that, but freestyle is a little more extravagant, with some creative flourishes permitted. For example, the dog doesn't have to stick so closely to the handler in the traditional heelwork position, but can 'dance' independently and perform various tricks to wow the crowd.

It's great fun – but harder than it looks! Your Russell will certainly enjoy the training with you, and, being the extrovert souls they are, most thrive in the ring.

Therapy work

A less energetic hobby is therapy work, where you take your Russell to meet people who could benefit from canine interaction. For example, in residential homes for the elderly, hospices and children's centres.

It is hugely rewarding to see the joy that a dog can bring to those that are not able to enjoy canine companionship, and there are many benefits. For example, the visits can encourage the elderly to talk about any past pets they have owned.

There are physical benefits to stroking a pet and an increased sense of wellbeing.

Most Russells are sociable extroverts and thrive on the attention, so it is bound to be a well-received hobby for your terrier.

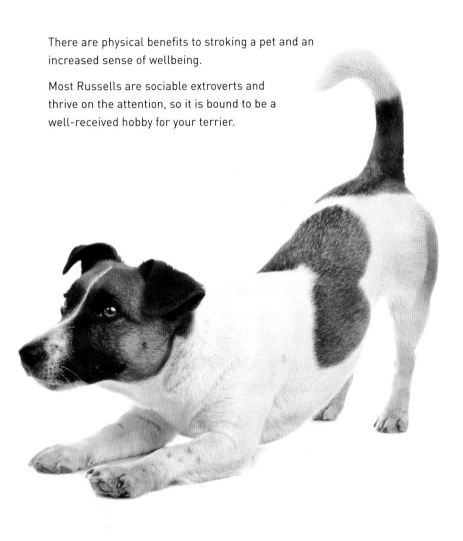

Health care

We are fortunate that the Russell Terrier is a healthy dog and, with good routine care, a well-balanced diet, and sufficient exercise, most will experience few health problems.

However, it is your responsibility to put a program of preventative health care in place – and this should start from the moment your puppy, or older dog, arrives in his new home.

Vaccinations

Dogs are subject to a number of contagious diseases. In the old days, these were killers, and resulted in heartbreak for many owners. Vaccinations have now been developed, and the occurrence of the major infectious diseases is now very rare. However, this will only remain the case if all pet owners follow a strict policy of vaccinating their dogs.

There are vaccinations available for the following diseases:

Adenovirus: This affects the liver; affected dogs have a classic 'blue eye'.

Distemper: A viral disease which causes chest and gastro-intestinal damage. The brain may also be affected, leading to fits and paralysis.

Parvovirus: Causes severe gastro enteritis, and most commonly affects puppies.

Leptospirosis: This bacterial disease is carried by rats and affects many mammals, including humans. It causes liver and kidney damage.

Rabies: A virus that affects the nervous system and is invariably fatal. The first signs are abnormal behavior when the infected dog may bite another animal or a person. Paralysis and death follow. Vaccination is compulsory in most countries. In the UK, dogs travelling overseas must be vaccinated.

Kennel Cough: There are several strains of Kennel Cough, but they all result in a harsh, dry, cough. This disease is rarely fatal; in fact most dogs make a good recovery within a matter of weeks and show few signs of ill health while they are affected. However, kennel cough is highly infectious among dogs that live together so, for this reason, most boarding kennels will insist that your dog is protected by the vaccine, which is given as nose drops.

Lyme Disease: This is a bacterial disease transmitted by ticks (see page 170). The first signs are limping, but the heart, kidneys and nervous system can also be affected. The ticks that transmit the disease occur in specific regions, such as the north-east states of the USA, some of the southern states, California and the upper Mississippi region. Lyme disease is till rare in the UK so vaccinations are not routinely offered.

Vaccination program

In the UK, vaccinations are routinely given for distemper, adenovirus, leptospirosis and parvo virus. In the USA, the American Animal Hospital Association advises vaccination for core diseases, which they list as distemper, adenovirus, parvovirus and rabies. The requirement for vaccinating for non-core diseases – leptospirosis, Lyme disease and kennel cough – should be assessed depending on a dog's individual risk and his likely exposure to the disease.

In most cases, a puppy will start his vaccinations at around eight weeks of age, with the second part given a fortnight later. However, this does vary depending on the individual policy of veterinary practices, and the incidence of disease in your area.

You should also talk to your vet about whether to give annual booster vaccinations. This depends on an individual dog's levels of immunity, and how long a particular vaccine remains effective.

Parasites

No matter how well you look after your Russell Terrier, you will have to accept that parasites – internal and external – are ever present, and you need to take preventative action.

Internal parasites: As the name suggests, these parasites live inside your dog. Most will find a home in the digestive tract, but there is also a parasite that lives in the heart. If infestation is unchecked, a dog's health will be severely jeopardized, but routine preventative treatment is simple and effective.

External parasites: These parasites live on your dog's body – in his skin and fur, and sometimes in his ears.

Roundworm

This is found in the small intestine, and signs of infestation will be a poor coat, a pot belly, diarrhoea and lethargy. Pregnant mothers should be treated, but it is almost inevitable that the worms will be

All puppies should be routinely treated for roundworm.

passed on to the puppies. For this reason, a breeder will start a worming program, which you will need to continue. Ask your vet for advice on treatment, which will need to continue throughout your dog's life.

Tapeworm

Infection occurs when fleas and lice are ingested; the adult worm takes up residence in the small intestine, releasing mobile segments (which contain eggs) that can be seen in a dog's feces as small rice-like grains. The only other obvious sign of infestation is irritation of the anus. Again, routine preventative treatment is required throughout your Russell's life.

Heartworm

This parasite is transmitted by mosquitoes, and so will only occur where these insects thrive. A warm environment is needed for the parasite to develop, so it is more likely to be present in areas with a warm, humid climate. However, it is found in all parts of the USA, although its prevalence does vary. At present, heartworm is rarely seen in the UK.

Heartworms live in the right side of the heart and larvae can grow up to 14 in (35 cm) in length. A dog with heartworm is at severe risk from heart failure, so preventative treatment, as advised by your vet, is essential. Dogs living in the USA should also have regular tests to check for the presence of infection.

Lungworm

Lungworm, or *Angiostrongylus vasorum*, is a parasite that lives in the heart and major blood vessels supplying the lungs. It can cause many problems, such as breathing difficulties, excessive bleeding, sickness and diarrhoea, seizures, and can even be fatal. The parasite is carried by slugs and snails, and in their trails, and the dog becomes infected when ingesting these, often accidentally when rummaging through undergrowth.

Lungworm is not common, but it is on the increase and a responsible owner should be aware of it.

Fortunately, it is easily preventable and even affected dogs usually make a full recovery if treated early enough. Your vet will be able to advise you on the risks in your area and what form of treatment may be required.

Fleas

A dog may carry dog fleas, cat fleas, and even human fleas. The flea stays on the dog only long enough to have a blood meal and to breed, but its presence will result in itching and scratching. If your dog has an allergy to fleas – which is usually a reaction to the flea's saliva – he will scratch himself until he is raw.

Spot-on treatment, which should be administered on a routine basis, is easy to use and highly effective on all types of fleas. You can also treat your dog with a spray or with insecticidal shampoo. Bear in mind that the whole environment your dog lives in will need to be sprayed, and all other pets living in your home will also need to be treated.

How to detect fleas

You may suspect your dog has fleas, but how can you be sure? There are two methods to try.

Run a fine comb through your dog's coat, and see if you can detect the presence of fleas on the skin, or clinging to the comb. Alternatively, sit your dog on some white paper and rub his back. This will dislodge feces from the fleas, which will be visible as small brown specks. To double check, shake the specks on to some damp cotton wool (cotton). Flea feces consists of the dried blood taken from the host, so if the specks turn a lighter shade of red, you know your dog has fleas.

Ticks

These are blood-sucking parasites most frequently found in rural area where sheep or deer are present. The main danger is their ability to pass Lyme disease to both dogs and humans. Lyme disease is prevalent in some areas of the USA (see page 165), although it is still rare in the UK. The treatment you give your dog for fleas is said to work for ticks, but you should discuss the best product to use with your vet.

How to remove a tick

If you spot a tick on your dog, do not try to pluck it off as you risk leaving the hard mouth parts embedded in his skin. The best way to remove a tick is to use a fine pair of tweezers, or you can buy a tick hook. Grasp the tick head firmly and then pull the tick straight out from the skin. If you are using a tick remover, check the instructions, as some recommend a circular twist when pulling. When you have removed the tick, clean the area with mild soap and water.

Ear mites

These parasites live in the outer ear canal. The signs of infestation are a brown, waxy discharge, and your dog will continually shake his head and scratch his ear. If you suspect your Russell has ear mites, a visit to the vet will be needed so that medicated ear drops can be prescribed.

Fur mites

These small, white parasites are visible to the naked eye and are often referred to as 'walking dandruff'. They cause a scurfy coat and mild itchiness. However, they are zoonotic – transferable to humans – so prompt treatment with an insecticide prescribed by your vet is essential.

Harvest mites

These are picked up from the undergrowth, and can be seen as a bright orange patch on the webbing between the toes, although this can also be found elsewhere on the body, such as on the ear flaps. Treatment is effective with the appropriate insecticide.

Skin mites

There are two types of parasite that burrow into a dog's skin. Demodex canis is transferred from a mother to her pups while they are feeding. Treatment is with a topical preparation, and sometimes antibiotics are needed.

The other skin mite is sarcoptes scabiei, which causes intense itching and hair loss. It is highly contagious, so all dogs in a household will need to be treated, which involves repeated bathing with a medicated shampoo.

Common ailments

As with all living animals, dogs can be affected by a variety of ailments. Most can be treated effectively after consulting with your vet, who will prescribe appropriate medication and will advise you on how to care for your dog's needs.

Here are some of the more common problems that could affect your Russell Terrier, with advice on how to deal with them.

Anal glands

These are two small sacs on either side of the anus, which produce a dark-brown secretion that dogs use when they mark their territory. The anal glands should empty every time a dog defecates but if they become blocked or impacted, a dog will experience increasing discomfort. He may nibble at his rear end, or 'scoot' his bottom along the ground to relieve the irritation.

Treatment involves a trip to the vet who will empty the glands manually. It is important to do this without delay or infection may occur.

Dental problems

Good dental hygiene will do much to minimize problems with gum infection and tooth decay. If tartar accumulates to the extent that you cannot remove it by brushing, the vet will need to intervene. In a situation such as this, an anesthetic will need to be administered so the tartar can be removed manually.

Diarrhoea

There are many reasons why a dog has diarrhoea, but most commonly it is the result of scavenging, a sudden change of diet, or an adverse reaction to a particular type of food.

If your dog is suffering from diarrhoea, the first step is to withdraw food for a day. It is important that he does not dehydrate, so make sure that fresh drinking water is available. However, drinking too much can increase the diarrhoea, which may be accompanied with vomiting, so limit how much he drinks at any one time.

After allowing the stomach to rest, feed a bland diet, such as white fish or chicken with boiled rice, for a few days. In most cases, your dog's motions will return to normal and you can resume usual feeding, although this should be done gradually.

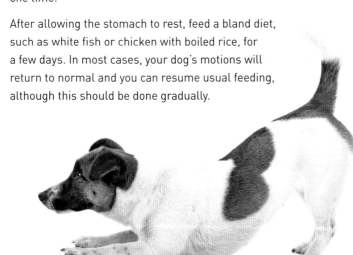

However, if this fails to work and the diarrhoea persists for more than a few days, you should consult you vet. Your dog may have an infection which needs to be treated with antibiotics, or the diarrhoea may indicate some other problem which needs expert diagnosis.

Ear infections

The Russell Terrier has V-shaped ears which are carried close to the head. They are small and neat, which means they are not vulnerable to injury, but they can be prone to ear infections.

A healthy ear is clean with no sign of redness or inflammation, and no evidence of a waxy brown discharge or a foul odor. If you see your dog scratching his ear, shaking his head, or holding one ear at an odd angle, you will need to consult your vet.

The most likely causes are ear mites, an infection, or there may a foreign body, such as a grass seed, trapped in the ear.

Depending on the cause, treatment is with medicated ear drops, possibly containing antibiotics. If a foreign body is suspected, the vet will need to carry our further investigations.

Eye problems

The Russell Terrier has almond shaped eyes, which do not protrude, so trauma to the eye is rare. But if your Russell's eyes look red and sore, he may be suffering from conjunctivitis. This may, or may not be accompanied with a watery or a crusty discharge. Conjunctivitis can be caused by a bacterial or viral infection, it could be the result of an injury, or it could be an adverse reaction to pollen.

You will need to consult your vet for a correct diagnosis, but in the case of an infection, treatment with medicated eye drops is effective.

Conjunctivitis may also be the first sign of more serious inherited eye problems (see page 186).

In some instances, a dog may suffer from dry, itchy eye, which he may further injure through scratching. This condition, known as keratoconjunctivitis sicca, may be inherited.

Foreign bodies

In the home, puppies – and some older dogs – cannot resist chewing anything that looks interesting. The toys you choose for your dog should be suitably robust to withstand damage, but children's toys can be irresistible. Some dogs will chew – and swallow – anything from socks, tights,

and any other items from the laundry basket to golf balls and stones from the garden. Obviously, these items are indigestible and could cause an obstruction in your dog's intestine, which is potentially lethal.

The signs to look for are vomiting, and a tucked up posture. The dog will often be restless and will look as though he is in pain.

In this situation, you must get your dog to the vet without delay as surgery will be needed to remove the obstruction.

Heatstroke

The Russell Terrier is full of energy and sometimes he is not the best judge of his own wellbeing. On hot days, make sure your dog always has access to shady areas, and wait for a cooler part of the day before going for a walk. Be extra careful if you leave your Jack Russell in the car, as the temperature can rise dramatically – even on a cloudy day. Heatstroke can happen very rapidly, and unless you are able lower your dog's temperature, it can be fatal.

If your Russell appears to be suffering from heatstroke, lie him flat and try to reduce his core body temperature by wrapping him in cool towels. A dog should not be immersed in cold water as this will cause the blood vessels to constrict, impeding heat dissipation. As soon as he has made some recovery, take him to the vet, where cold intravenous fluids can be administered.

Lameness/limping

There are a wide variety of reasons why a dog can go lame – from a simple muscle strain, to a fracture, ligament damage, or more complex problems with the joints. If you are concerned about your dog, do not delay in seeking help.

As your Russell becomes more elderly, he may suffer from arthritis, which you will see as general stiffness, particularly when he gets up after resting. It will help if you ensure his bed is in a warm draught-free location, and if your Russell gets wet after exercise, you must dry him thoroughly.

If your Russell seems to be in pain, consult your vet who will be able to help with pain relief.

Skin problems

If your dog is scratching or nibbling at his skin, first check he is free from fleas (see page?). There are other external parasites which cause itching and hair loss, but you will need a vet to help you find the culprit.

An allergic reaction is another major cause of skin problems. It can be quite an undertaking to find the cause of the allergy, and you will need to follow your vet's advice, which often requires eliminating specific ingredients from the diet, as well as looking at environmental factors (See page 169).

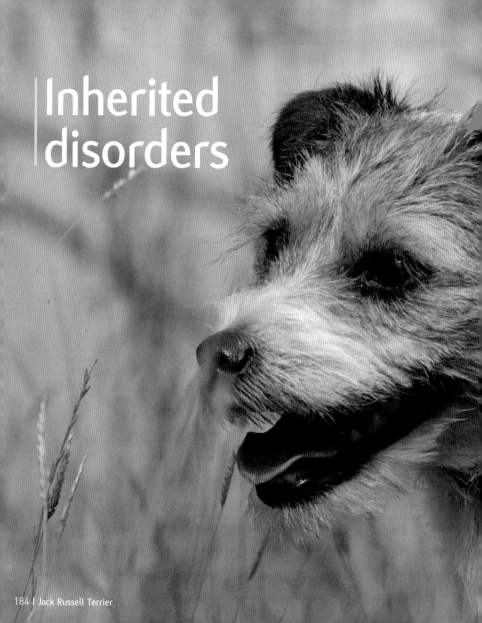

Inherited
disorders

The Russell Terrier does have a few breed-related disorders, which can be passed on from one generation to the next. Although breeders strive to eliminate these problems from their bloodlines, it is important to research thoroughly before buying a puppy.

There are now recognized screening tests to enable breeders to check for affected individuals and hence reduce the prevalence of these diseases within the breed. DNA testing is also becoming more widely available, and as research into the different genetic diseases progresses, more DNA tests are being developed.

Hereditary cataracts

Cataracts are an opacification of the lens of the eye, which may be very small or involve the entire lens. This can happen at any age in the Russell Terrier in the hereditary form. Like humans, cataracts in dogs can also develop with age. Once a cataract has developed, surgery is the treatment of choice for removal.

Primary lens luxation

In this painful, inherited eye disorder, the lens of
the eye luxates (becomes loose, moves, or even
detaches) and can cause blindness. The vision
cannot always be saved once primary lens luxation is
identified. It usually strikes from two to six years of
age onwards, and both sexes can get it, although it
is more common in females. One eye will be affected
first, often followed by another (with an interval that
can be a few weeks, to even a few years).

Breeding stock should be tested using the Canine
Eye Registration Foundation in the US, or the
combined scheme run by the British Veterinary
Association, the Kennel Club and the International
Sheep Dog Society in the UK.

Research is on-going to find a DNA test which will
make detection easier.

Medial patellar luxation

This is condition where the patella (kneecap)
becomes displaced medially from its normal
position. Clinical signs can vary from an intermittent
luxation with skipping or slight lameness, to
permanent luxation with severe lameness and
displacement of the leg muscles. The condition

can worsen with time. If very mild, cases may be managed with restricted exercise and weight control. More severe cases require surgery and will inevitably suffer some form of degenerative joint disease in the affected joint.

Legg-Calvé-Perthes disease

This is where avascular necrosis (degeneration) of the femoral head and neck (top of the thigh bone) occurs, resulting in collapse of the hip joint and osteoarthritis. Mechanism of inheritance is unknown. It is usually seen in younger Russell Terriers and presents as progressively worsening lameness of the hind limbs.

X-rays are usually indicated to help diagnose the problem and surgery to remove the affected bone. Once the damaged bone is removed, the lameness usually resolves and the dog can live a normal, healthy lifestyle.

Cerebellar ataxia

This is a neurological disorder seen in Russell Terrier pups from two to four weeks old and is caused by progressive degeneration of the cerebellum (part of the brain which controls fine muscle movement and balance). This causes a number of clinical signs from lack of co-ordination while walking, stumbling, extended legs and a tremor of the head to an inability to stand. The signs worsen with time and there is no cure.

Summing up

It may give the pet owner cause for concern to find about health problems that may affect their dog. But it is important to bear in mind that acquiring some basic knowledge is an asset as it will allow you to spot signs of trouble at an early stage. Early diagnosis is very often the means to the most effective treatment.

We are fortunate that the Russell Terrier is a tough, hardy breed, and in most cases, owners can look forward to enjoying many years of companionship with this exceptional little terrier.

Useful addresses

Breed & Kennel Clubs
Please contact your Kennel Club to obtain contact information about breed clubs in your area.

UK
The Kennel Club (UK)
1 Clarges Street London, W1J 8AB
Telephone: 0870 606 6750
Fax: 0207 518 1058
Web: www.thekennelclub.org.uk

USA
American Kennel Club (AKC)
5580 Centerview Drive, Raleigh, NC 27606.
Telephone: 919 233 9767
Fax: 919 233 3627
Email: info@akc.org
Web: www.akc.org

United Kennel Club (UKC)
100 E Kilgore Rd, Kalamazoo,
MI 49002-5584, USA.
Tel: 269 343 9020
Fax: 269 343 7037
Web:www.ukcdogs.com/

Australia
Australian National Kennel Council (ANKC)
The Australian National Kennel Council is the administrative body for pure breed canine affairs in Australia. It does not, however, deal directly with dog exhibitors, breeders or judges. For information pertaining to breeders, clubs or shows, please contact the relevant State or Territory Body.

International
Fédération Cynologique Internationalé (FCI)
Place Albert 1er, 13, B-6530 Thuin, Belgium.
Tel: +32 71 59.12.38
Fax: +32 71 59.22.29
Web: www.fci.be/

Training and behavior
UK
Association of Pet Dog Trainers
Telephone: 01285 810811
Web: http://www.apdt.co.uk

Canine Behaviour
Association of Pet Behaviour Counsellors
Telephone: 01386 751151
Web: http://www.apbc.org.uk/

USA
Association of Pet Dog Trainers
Tel: 1 800 738 3647
Web: www.apdt.com/

American College of Veterinary Behaviorists
Web: http://dacvb.org/

American Veterinary Society of Animal Behavior
Web: www.avsabonline.org/

Australia
APDT Australia Inc
Web: www.apdt.com.au

For details of regional behaviorists, contact the relevant State or Territory Controlling Body.

Agility Club
http://www.agilityclub.co.uk/

British Flyball Association
Telephone: 01628 829623
Web: http://www.flyball.org.uk/

USA
North American Dog Agility Council
Web: www.nadac.com/

North American Flyball Association, Inc.
Tel/Fax: 800 318 6312
Web: www.flyball.org/

Australia
Agility Dog Association of Australia
Tel: 0423 138 914
Web: www.adaa.com.au/

NADAC Australia
Web: www.nadacaustralia.com/

Australian Flyball Association
Tel: 0407 337 939
Web: www.flyball.org.au/

International
World Canine Freestyle Organisation
Tel: (718) 332-8336
Web: www.worldcaninefreestyle.org

Health
UK
British Small Animal Veterinary Association
Tel: 01452 726700
Web: http://www.bsava.com/

Royal College of Veterinary Surgeons
Tel: 0207 222 2001
Web: www.rcvs.org.uk

www.dogbooksonline.co.uk/healthcare/

Alternative Veterinary Medicine Centre
Tel: 01367 710324
Web: www.alternativevet.org/

USA
American Veterinary Medical Association
Tel: 800 248 2862
Web: www.avma.org

American College of Veterinary Surgeons
Tel: 301 916 0200
Toll Free: 877 217 2287
Web: www.acvs.org/

Canine Eye Registration Foundation
The Veterinary Medical DataBases
1717 Philo Rd, PO Box 3007,
Urbana, IL 61803-3007
Tel: 217-693-4800
Fax: 217-693-4801
Web: http://www.vmdb.org/cerf.html

Orthopaedic Foundation of Animals
2300 E Nifong Boulevard
Columbia, Missouri, 65201-3806
Tel: 573 442-0418
Fax: 573 875-5073
Web: http://www.offa.org/

American Holistic Veterinary Medical
Association
Tel: 410 569 0795
Web: www.ahvma.org/

Australia
Australian Small Animal Veterinary
Association
Tel: 02 9431 5090
Web: www.asava.com.au

Australian Veterinary Association
Tel: 02 9431 5000
Web: www.ava.com.au

Australian College Veterinary Scientists
Tel: 07 3423 2016
Web: http://acvsc.org.au

Australian Holistic Vets
Web: www.ahv.com.au/